Y0-DJM-320

BEFORE YOU GO

WISDOM TO TAKE WITH YOU

PRESENTED TO

BY

DATE

Lifeway Press®
Brentwood, Tennessee

ISBN 978-1-0877-8485-4
Item 005842357
Dewey Decimal Classification Number: 242
Subject Heading: DEVOTIONAL LITERATURE / BIBLE STUDY AND TEACHING / GOD

Printed in the United States of America.

Student Ministry Publishing
Lifeway Resources
200 Powell Place, Suite 100
Brentwood, Tennessee 37027

We believe that the Bible has God for its author; salvation for its end; truth, without any mixture of error, for its matter; and that all Scripture is totally true and trustworthy. To review Lifeway's doctrinal guideline, please visit https://www.lifeway.com/about/doctrinal-guidelines.

Unless otherwise noted, all Scripture quotations are taken from the Christian Standard Bible®, Copyright © 2017 by Holman Bible Publishers. Used by permission. Christian Standard Bible® and CSB® are federally registered trademarks of Holman Bible Publishers.

PUBLISHING TEAM

Director, NextGen Ministries
Chuck Peters

Manager, Small Group Resources
Karen Daniel

Writers
Alecia Bryant, April-Lyn Caouette, Kyle Cravens, Tega Faafa Taylor, Nancy Farag, Claudia Hallquist, Taylor Heatherly, Justin McDowell, Nightingale Ngo, and Zoë Wilson

Content Editor
Kyle Wiltshire

Production Editor
April-Lyn Caouette

Graphic Designer
Shiloh Stufflebeam

TABLE OF CONTENTS

INTRO

This is an exciting time in your life! You've just reached a big milestone and are about to enter the next phase in your journey. During the next few weeks, you'll probably hear more words than you'll be able to remember about how important this transition is. And for good reason: this truly is a crucial season in your life. The decisions you make within the next few years will shape so much moving forward.

But here's the hard reality: too many people your age come to this huge transition and change something that doesn't need to be changed. When many students graduate from high school, they unfortunately also end up walking away from church. In fact, 66 percent of students who were active in church during their high school years were not after they graduated.[1] We don't want that to be you.

In this devotional, we have collected what we consider to be some of the most important verses in the Bible about how to stay firmly rooted in your faith. As you leave high school, we hope that you will internalize these words of wisdom and live by them as you travel from this stage of your life and on to the next.

This book was a team effort: it has ten writers, all of whom have leadership positions within the Lifeway Students team. They represent a variety of perspectives within our team: camps, publishing, and even marketing. But we all share the same passion: to see you grow in your relationship with Jesus.

This little book is a love letter from us to you. We are proud of your accomplishment! We're cheering for you and praying that God richly blesses you as you move to the next phase in life.

GETTING STARTED

This devotional contains thirty days of content, broken down into sections. Each day is divided into three elements—**discover**, **delight**, and **display**—to help you grow in your faith.

DISCOVER

This section helps you examine Scripture in light of who God is and determine what it says about your identity in relationship to Him. Included here are the daily Bible reading and key verses, along with illustrations and commentary to guide you as you learn more about God's Word.

DELIGHT

In this section, you'll be challenged by questions and activities that help you see how God is alive and active in every detail of His Word and your life.

DISPLAY

Here's where you take action. This section calls you to apply what you've learned through each day.

> **Each day also includes a prayer activity at the conclusion of the devotion.**

Throughout the devotional, you'll also find extra items to help you connect with the topic personally, such as Scripture memory verses and interactive articles.

PHILIPPIANS 1:3-11

Philippians was written by the apostle Paul while he was in prison. Despite his circumstances, his faith in Jesus never wavered. In fact, he used his time in chains to encourage others to continue to grow in their faith. The next few years can be a great time of growth for you, but you must use the time that the Lord gives you wisely. Philippians 1:3-11 can help you know how to use that time to the fullest.

WRITERS:

Nightingale Ngo (Days 1–3)
Camp Registration and Customer Specialist

Justin McDowell (Days 4–6)
Ministry Event Specialist, Student Life Camps

April-Lyn Caouette (Days 7–9)
Production Editor, Student Publishing

WITH GRATITUDE

READ PHILIPPIANS 1:3.

I give thanks to my God for every remembrance of you . . .
— Philippians 1:3

DISCOVER

Thanksgiving is my favorite holiday. Not only does it involve an abundance of delicious food, but it is a day set aside for one purpose: giving thanks.

It is easy to give thanks when we're going through wonderful and happy seasons in our lives. It takes more effort when we are going through tough times. However, the apostle Paul (the author of today's verse) was grateful and joyful in any circumstance, even when he was in prison for sharing the gospel. How was he able to give thanks while sitting in a jail cell? In Philippians 1:3, Paul is very specific about whom he gives thanks to and the nature of their relationship—Paul directs his thanks to "my God," revealing a personal, intimate connection between them.

Paul is also very specific about whom he is thankful for. The church in Philippi supported Paul financially and emotionally, and he knew that even though he was in jail, they would continue to support him. They weren't afraid of being associated with him. Paul acknowledged that God gave him this community to encourage him. He knew God was with him in his prison cell because He had been faithful to provide believers who would encourage Paul in his darkest moments.

God longs to be the Lord and Savior of your life, just as He was for Paul. How do you see your relationship with God?

In what ways do you desire to grow closer to Him?

What is one action step you can take in the next phase of your life to continue growing in your relationship with God?

Whom has God brought alongside you to encourage you in your journey? When you are miles away from home, you may feel a tinge of loneliness. The church of Philippi brought joy to Paul while he was physically in a very dark and lonely place. Write down names of people who bring you feelings of gratitude every time you think of them. Send them a note or text telling them how thankful you are for them.

Come before the Lord and thank Him for the people He brought to encourage you, particularly as you look back on your time in high school. As you thank Him, pray that the Lord would encourage those people as they have encouraged you.

KNOWING HIM

READ PHILIPPIANS 1:3-4.

. . . always praying with joy for all of you in my every prayer . . .
— Philippians 1:4

DISCOVER

Some years ago, a friend told me that whenever someone comes to his mind, he pauses from whatever he is doing and says a prayer for that person. He may not know why the Lord brought that person to mind, but he wants to be obedient and faithful in prayer.

Prayer was an important part of Paul's life, too. He wrote about prayer many times in his letters, and in Philippians 1:3, he referred to "my God," showing an intimacy in his relationship with the Lord. Prayer allows us direct access to God; it allows us to know His heart and to seek Him and His guidance in our daily lives. Prayer is how we grow our relationship with God.

The church in Philippi was at the forefront of Paul's mind, and he continually prayed for them. Not only that, but he prayed "with joy." Not even being in a jail cell dampened his spirits! Paul knew that God was his ultimate sustainer and that God used the Philippian church to encourage him. For Paul, praying for the believers in Philippi was joyful, not routine or forced. It was a joy for Paul to come before the Lord and present his requests, and it was a joy for him to pray for others. He knew God was working in their lives, just as He was working in Paul's, no matter the circumstances.

What is your attitude toward prayer?

Do you struggle to pray and see it only as a duty or task? Or is prayer an intimate time to come before your God with what is on your heart? Explain.

What is one step you can take to grow in prayer as you enter a new stage of life?

Spend a few minutes today in prayer. It doesn't have to be long or structured—just a few minutes without distractions for you to bring your heart's affections and desires to the Lord. He longs for you to know Him! Then, as you go about your day today, when someone comes to mind, say a prayer for him or her. Sometimes the person who comes to mind may be someone with whom you are frustrated or someone you don't have a good relationship with. It may not bring you joy to pray for that person, but praying for him or her at that moment may help you both.

Today, seek the Lord by saying a prayer for those who come into your mind throughout the day. You may never know why God brought these people to mind and you may never know how much your prayers are needed. Be faithful to lift others up to our mighty, wonderful, powerful God.

RIDE OR DIE

READ PHILIPPIANS 1:3-5.

. . . because of your partnership in the gospel from the first day until now.
— Philippians 1:5

DISCOVER

You know the phrase "ride or die," right? It's an exaggerated way to identify the people in your life who stick with you (and you with them) in good times and bad. So, who immediately comes to mind when you think of your "ride or die"?

Knowing that someone has our back no matter what can bring us encouragement, confidence, and comfort. For Paul, the believers in the church of Philippi were "ride or die" friends. They had faithfully joined him in spreading the gospel and their partnership brought him encouragement and joy, even as he was in a dark and lonely time. Paul knew their support also meant putting themselves in danger: since he was in prison for sharing the gospel, it was very possible that associating with him could cause trouble for them, including persecution. But regardless of the possible consequences, they weren't afraid. Instead, they were committed to supporting Paul and the work of spreading the gospel.

Of all the churches to whom Paul wrote letters, he was most inspired and encouraged by the faithfulness of the church at Philippi. Their unwavering support reminded him of God's goodness and provision, and it reminded him that he was never alone.

What are some of the most important characteristics you look for in a "ride or die" relationship?

What can you do in the next phase of your life to be the type of friend who is faithful to others and committed to healthy, deep, godly relationships?

Think about your middle school and high school years. Who have been your partners in the gospel—the people who have taught you about Jesus and with whom you have grown in your faith? This could include your youth minister, a small group leader, someone who led a club or group you belonged to (like FCA or Young Life), a family member, or even the pastor at your church. Let these people know what they've meant to you in your walk with Jesus and what they mean to you now as you start this new chapter in your journey. Then thank God for bringing them into your life, and ask Him how you can serve them well.

As you spend time with God in prayer today, thank Him for the joy of having people who support you unconditionally—near or far. Ask Him to bless and guard them, and ask Him how you can encourage them.

FROM START TO FINISH

READ PHILIPPIANS 1:3-6.

I am sure of this, that he who started a good work in you will carry it on to completion until the day of Christ Jesus.
— Philippians 1:6

DISCOVER

Every January, motivated individuals hit the gym, ready to get in shape after setting their New Year's resolutions. However, it doesn't take long for the gym crowds to start shrinking again. Out of all the people who vow to exercise more, read more, or eat healthier, nearly 80 percent of people who make New Year's resolutions have given up on them by February.[2] The reality is, it can be difficult for any of us to complete what we've begun. But unlike us, God always finishes what He starts.

In today's verses, Paul is encouraging the Philippian Christians by reminding them of the assurance they have in Jesus. Who started a good work in the lives of the Philippians, according to Paul? God, the Creator of the heavens and the earth! And what is the good work God began in them? Salvation through Jesus Christ. The same God who had transformed their lives would continue to be with them and for them, changing them to be like Jesus. God will carry out this work in every believer until Christ returns. This proclamation wasn't just a theory Paul offered to comfort them; he was confident of Jesus's saving work in their lives.

If you know Jesus as Lord, God has started a good work in you as well. Nothing in this world can stop God from completing His work in your life. Regardless of what you face ahead, God will continue to work in and through you.

Do you share Paul's confidence about God's work in your life? If so, where does this confidence come from? If not, what is holding you back from embracing this truth?

Think of people in your life who need to hear this encouragement. How can you share with them about the assurance they can find in Jesus?

Sometimes it can be difficult to sense what God is doing in our lives. Life gets busy and difficult, and we wonder if God is still at work. Paul, who was no stranger to this type of thinking, knew that God remains sovereign over all, including our current circumstances. God does not leave us after we decide to place our faith in Jesus. He continues to be at work in our lives every day. Reflect on how God has been working in your life lately, and brief write down what you discover in the space below.

Thank God for the saving work He has already done in your life through His Son, Jesus, and thank Him for continuing to be at work in you. Pray that you would remain confident of His presence in your life, regardless of the ups and downs.

MEMORY VERSE

I AM SURE OF
THIS, THAT HE
WHO STARTED A
GOOD WORK IN YOU
WILL CARRY IT ON
TO COMPLETION
UNTIL THE DAY OF
CHRIST JESUS.

— PHILIPPIANS 1:6

PARTNERS IN GRACE

READ PHILIPPIANS 1:3-7.

Indeed, it is right for me to think this way about all of you, because I have you in my heart, and you are all partners with me in grace, both in my imprisonment and in the defense and confirmation of the gospel.
— Philippians 1:7

DISCOVER

Have you ever been part of a team? Maybe you've been on a sports team, a debate team, or in a musical ensemble. Think of the connection you felt with the others on that team because of your shared experience. Paul experienced this kind of connection with the Philippians so much that he viewed them as "partners in grace."

Philippi was a Roman colony, and even though it was about eight hundred miles from Rome, its culture was still heavily influenced by Roman rule, and it was home to many Roman military personnel. It was not easy for Philippian Christians to follow the way of Jesus rather than the way of Rome. Yet the Philippians continued to follow Jesus and support Paul in his ministry. And Paul understood the hardship they faced; after all, he himself had been imprisoned for proclaiming the gospel and was writing this letter to them from that prison.

Paul knew that his situation was not unique to him: any follower of Christ will endure hardship. While you probably will not be thrown in jail like Paul was, you will inevitably struggle because of your faith. You may be in a place where there are not many believers around. Some of your peers may give you a hard time for your faith. While these moments can be isolating, remember that you are not alone. Fellow believers—friends, family, ministers—are walking alongside you. And as the phrase "partners in grace" implies, God continues to be with you as well.

When have you experienced hardship because of your faith in Jesus? How did you respond?

Whom have you relied on when you were going through a tough time? Have others been able to rely on you when they're struggling? Why or why not?

We all need Christian community. Fellow believers support us and help us continue to live like Jesus. Whether you plan to start college, travel to new places, start a new job, or continue a job you already had, think of ways you can find Christian community wherever you are. If you're going to college, research the campus ministries at school. If you're moving to a new place for school or work, research the area churches and make a list of a few you will visit. If you're not moving to a new area, be intentional about finding Christian community where you are. Join a ministry for college students, young professionals, or young adults in your church, and stay connected to Christian friends who will still be around.

Thank God for the "partners in grace" in your life. Thank Him for those who continue to support you. Ask God to continue to provide friends who can walk alongside you as you seek to faithfully follow Him.

LOVE YOU, MEAN IT

READ PHILIPPIANS 1:3-8.

*For God is my witness, how deeply I miss all of
you with the affection of Christ Jesus.*
— Philippians 1:8

DISCOVER

Being away from loved ones and missing them can be bittersweet. While
it's no fun to be apart from those we love, it does remind us that there
are people in our life who have cared for us. Today's verse shows us that
while Paul was locked up in a prison cell, he reflected on those he loved
and those who had walked alongside him throughout his journey.

The Philippians had supported Paul in his ministry and that support
continued while he was in prison. While Paul certainly was thankful for
their personal support, his gratitude for them ran much deeper. The
Philippians weren't just his supporters—they were his brothers and sisters
in Christ. The Philippians' support for him was secondary to their living
out and proclaiming the gospel. Paul and the believers in Philippi were
united through their common devotion to Jesus. Paul was so adamant in
his affection for the Philippians that he said God Himself could testify to
this fact. His deep affection didn't originate from within him; it was the
love of Jesus Christ that Paul exemplified.

Paul's love for his friends was a reflection of Jesus's love for us. Paul
and the Philippians both displayed His sacrificial love through their
mutual concern for one another. As followers of Christ, we are called
to demonstrate the love of Jesus by loving one another, whether it's a
close friend or a stranger—and we're called to do this every moment of
every day.

Who are some people in your life who have shown you the love of Christ? How have they shown you that they love you?

How have you displayed the love of Jesus to your friends and family?

What can you do in the next step of your life to continue to cultivate loving, Christlike relationships?

Paul and the Philippian Christians were able to love one another despite the distance (and prison cell) between them. If they could love and support each other two thousand years ago without modern technology, you can continue to show love to the family and friends who may soon live away from you. In the chart below, write ways you can demonstrate love to both those in your immediate community where you will be living and those you will be living away from.

My Immediate Community	Loved Ones Outside My Area

Pray the following:
Lord, thank You for the family and friends in my life. It is a blessing to have people in my life who love and care for me. I ask that You help me continue to show Your love to those already in my life as well as to those I have yet to meet. Amen.

THE RIGHT KIND OF LOVE

READ PHILIPPIANS 1:3-9.

And I pray this: that your love will keep on growing in knowledge and every kind of discernment . . .
— Philippians 1:9

DISCOVER

One chapter of your life is coming to a close and another is beginning. No matter what's next for you, the learning and growing doesn't stop here. In fact, this is the time when the real adventure begins. You'll be going to new places, meeting new people, and facing brand new challenges. You'll need to gain new skills and apply the tools you already have. Out of everything that you've learned, what's the one thing that will be most important for you to develop as you step out into the world? According to Paul, it's love.

You might be thinking: *Love? How is that going to help me get a job? How is that going to help me keep up my grades?* Well, maybe it won't, at least not directly. But the way you love will have an impact on every single person with whom you come into contact.

It's important to remember that Paul isn't talking about romantic love. He's talking about unconditional, self-sacrificial love—the same kind of love that led Jesus to the cross, and the kind of love that He calls His followers to show the world. This is the kind of love that we're called to show our neighbors, and it's the kind of love that should be at the root of a Christ follower's every action, every thought, and every moment.

Why do you think Paul places so much importance on growing in love?

What kind of impact could it have in your school, workplace, or community if you make it your first priority to show Christlike love to others every day?

What does it look like for us to use knowledge and discernment as we practice showing love to others?

It's easy to show love to others when things are going well, but we are called to show love even when we face challenges. Use the space below to make a short list of three to four challenging situations you might encounter in the next season of your life (such as competitive coworkers or loud dormitory parties when you're trying to study). Then, brainstorm a few ways that you can stay firm in your commitment to shine the light of God's love, even in these difficult scenarios.

Pray the following:
Jesus, thank You for coming to earth and showing us how to truly love the way that God loves us. Please help me to share Your love with the world as I step out into this new phase of my life. Amen.

MORE FREEDOM, MORE RESPONSIBILITY

READ PHILIPPIANS 1:3-10.

. . . so that you may approve the things that are superior and may be pure and blameless in the day of Christ . . .
— Philippians 1:10

DISCOVER

For the last few years, you may have felt like you were living in an in-between place: enjoying some freedoms you didn't have when you were younger but also feeling restricted by curfews, homework, and rules. Now you anxiously await the day when the world will treat you like an adult. That day is coming, if it hasn't already come.

When you turn eighteen, suddenly you will have a whole bunch of new things you're allowed to do, like vote, open your own bank account, enlist in the military, and rent an apartment. But with new permissions come new responsibilities: you're allowed to do more, but more is expected of you, too. With those permissions will come lots of choices. Thankfully, growing in Christlike love helps us to make the best choices.

The Greek word Paul used here for "pure" is related to the idea of holding something up to sunlight for inspection.[3] This is how Paul wants us to examine each situation we're in as we make decisions—and love is what will help us make those superior choices. When we are growing in love for God, we will want to make choices that align with His will. When we are growing in love for others, we will see that the choices we make affect everyone around us, and we will want to make choices that spread joy, goodness, and peace.

How does Christlike love help you make the best choices? If you can, give an example from your life.

What does it mean to be pure and blameless? What does this look like at work, at school, or with friends and family?

Some decisions have low stakes and are relatively easy to make, like what to eat for lunch. Other decisions take a bit more thought. What is a challenging decision you need to make soon? Write it down in the space below. Then, take a moment to invite the Holy Spirit to guide you as you work through the following exercise.

On the left-hand side of the chart, list a few of the top options you have (if you need more space, you can copy the chart to a separate piece of paper and add additional rows). Then start listing some of the pros and cons of each option. As you do, ask yourself the following questions: *How does this fit into God's will? How can this choice help me to grow into the person God has created me to be? How does this choice affect other people? How could my choice inspire or encourage others? How could this choice put me in a position to show love to others?*

I need to decide:

	Possible Choices:	**Pros:**	**Cons:**
OPTION 1:			
OPTION 2:			
OPTION 3:			

Pray the following:
God, when I have difficult decisions to make, please help me to make choices that are rooted in love. Thank You for giving me the privilege and responsibility of shining Your light in the world. I pray that I would always look to You for guidance, wisdom, and discernment. Amen.

RIGHTEOUS

READ PHILIPPIANS 1:3-11.

*...filled with the fruit of righteousness that comes through Jesus Christ
to the glory and praise of God.*
— Philippians 1:11

DISCOVER

Do you ever feel like people aren't taking you seriously? You may not have a spouse or a career or a house to take care of yet, but that doesn't make the stresses in your life any less real. Growing into adulthood is a challenge, and the worst part is that there isn't an instruction manual. But good news: Paul has some words of advice about how to let some of that stress go.

We've been talking about how Paul prayed for believers to grow in Christlike love and use that love to make good choices that honor God and bless others. In today's verse he says that we are able to do those things because we are "filled with the fruit of righteousness" (v. 11). What in the world is the fruit of righteousness? Righteousness is moral living that lines up with God's will. Paul describes it as something that is grown or produced, just as a healthy apple tree produces delicious fruit.

If righteous living is something that grows in us like fruit, what makes it grow? Righteous living "comes through Jesus Christ" (v. 11). When we walk closely with Him and learn His ways, He draws us closer and closer to Him. As He does, and as we learn to listen to the Holy Spirit within us, we grow in righteousness, and righteousness grows in us.

This doesn't mean you can do whatever you want and wait for Jesus to change your heart. But it does mean that instead of righteousness being just one more burden you have to carry, you can give it to Jesus. Let Him change your heart and show you how to follow Him. Talk to Him in prayer. Seek Him when life feels overwhelming. He will be with you every step of the way.

In your own words, what is righteousness? Have you ever thought of righteousness as something you had to do yourself? How does this verse challenge that idea?

Look back at our verses from days 7 and 8, and think about a challenge you're facing right now. How are love and righteousness connected to making decisions? How can these verses help you with your decisions and stresses?

If righteousness is a fruit that Jesus produces in us, what kind of fruit is it? In the space below, draw a simple tree with at least four or five branches. On each of those branches, draw a few pieces of fruit, and inside each of the fruit shapes, write a word related to righteousness. These could be words from our verses over the last few days, like "pure" or "love," or they could be words that describe righteousness, such as "goodness," "justice," or "honor." You might look up "righteousness" in a Bible dictionary or in the index of your Bible to see what other words come up. Now take a picture of your drawing or make a copy of it. Put this picture someplace you'll see it often. When you feel stressed or overwhelmed, look at your "tree of righteousness" to remember the kind of fruit that Jesus is creating in you to help you navigate life and bring God glory.

Pray the following:
God, life can be overwhelming, and often I try to do everything on my own. Thank You for promising to grow righteousness in me as I follow Jesus and listen to the guidance of the Holy Spirit. When I start feeling stressed, remind me that I should lean on You. Amen.

Autographs

You've probably collected a few yearbook autographs over the years—signatures with hearts and circles over the letter i, phone numbers, and social media handles. Usually, the people you ask to sign your yearbook mean something to you—even if they just sat next to you in the hardest class ever. So, let's think about the people who have meant something to you in your walk with Jesus. Choose some of these people and invite them to write a short note on this page to share words of wisdom with you for whatever phase of life you're walking into next.

JOHN 15

For three years, the apostle John traveled with Jesus, daily observing how He interacted with and loved others. When Jesus was crucified, John was the only one of His twelve disciples there. For the rest of his life, John lived by the words of John 15. He remained with Jesus and we would all do well to do the same.

WRITERS:

Alecia Bryant (Days 10–12)
Brand Owner/Content Editor, The Gospel Project

Nancy Farag (Days 13–15)
Event Coordinator, Student Life Camps

Nightingale Ngo (Day 16)
Camp Registration and Customer Specialist

Justin McDowell (Days 17–18)
Ministry Event Specialist, Student Life Camps

Claudia Hallquist (Days 19–20)
Ministry Event Specialist, FUGE Camps

Zoë Wilson (Days 21–22)
Camp Registration and Customer Specialist

DAY 10

THE ONLY VINE

READ JOHN 15:1-2.

"I am the true vine and my Father is the gardener."
— John 15:1

DISCOVER

Think about leaving the people you love most for an extended amount of time. What would you want them to know? What would you want them to remember? What would your last words be before leaving? John 15 is part of a section of Scripture we call the Farewell Discourse (see John 14–17), during which Jesus took the opportunity to tell His closest friends what He wanted them to remember before His crucifixion. Jesus knew the disciples would experience heartache and persecution, and He also knew they'd be vulnerable to doubt and disbelief. Here is what He commanded: *Stay connected to Me.* This command is ours as well.

Jesus urged the disciples to remain connected to Him in the same way that branches are connected to a vine. In verse 1, Jesus refers to Himself as the "true vine." This implies there are other vines out there that are false. There are many other vines we could connect ourselves to—things like popularity, social media, future plans, or relationships—but these vines won't keep us nourished. In fact, they'll always fail us—they'll always drain the life out of us. We can't depend on these vines because they were never meant to sustain us. While they may temporarily give us a jolt of happiness, they can never give us life.

If you're going to thrive spiritually and produce spiritual fruit, then you must remain connected to Jesus. He promises to sustain you; in fact, He is the only One who can. He also promises to prune you—a process by which He removes everything that drains you. This process can be difficult, but you can trust the Gardener's hands.

Why are false "vines" so appealing? How can they be deceiving?

What steps can you take each day to make sure you are connecting to Jesus, the one "true vine"?

Consider your own life: Are you growing spiritually? Are you producing fruit? Thinking through this will help you to identify the areas of your life that may need to be pruned.

DISPLAY

Make a list of some of the "false vines" you tend to be attracted to, then consider what attaching yourself to these vines may lead to. For example, attaching yourself to the "false vine" of popularity may only lead to comparison and placing your worth in others' opinions. Then consider the outcome of attaching yourself to Jesus, the true vine, instead.

False Vine:	What it Leads to:	Outcome of Remaining Connected to Christ:

Pray the following:
God, help me to see the ways I've attached myself to anything but You. Help me to identify the ways I've tried to find life apart from You. Prune me of anything that could rob me of abundant life and keep me from producing spiritual fruit. I trust Your hand to do what's best for me. Amen.

FRIENDSHIP WITH CHRIST

READ JOHN 15:3-4.

*"Remain in me, and I in you. Just as a branch is unable to
produce fruit by itself unless it remains on the vine,
neither can you unless you remain in me."*
— John 15:4

DISCOVER

True friendship is mutual, right? This means that both people are aware
of the friendship; it isn't one-sided. Maybe you've been in a one-sided
friendship before where you put in all the work. You were always the one
who reached out or initiated hanging out. If we're honest, this type of
"friendship" doesn't feel good; there's something missing. This is because
real friendship requires participation from both people.

As Jesus continued to talk with His disciples, there was one word He used
multiple times: "remain." This can also be translated as "abide," "dwell,"
or "stay." It's like Jesus was asking them to simply be with Him. Live with
Him. Dwell with Him. But here's the most amazing part: Jesus didn't just
tell them to remain; He said that He would remain also. Jesus's words
here remind us that we are invited into real, intimate friendship with Him!
However, we must make the choice every day to abide in Him. Each day,
we must make decisions that place us in His presence.

Jesus promised that once He left, He would send the Holy Spirit in His
place—a Friend, a Counselor, and the One who would convict us of our
sin. Jesus, God in the flesh, came to earth to dwell with humans, and
now He dwells within us through His Spirit. We can have true friendship
with the God of the universe! But we must do our part to remain in Him
and foster intimacy with Him. What a privilege that we get to call God
our friend!

How would you describe friendship? Why do we sometimes not apply this to our relationship with Jesus? How can you do so?

When has your relationship with God been one-sided? What steps can you take to grow your friendship with Him?

What does it reveal about God that He desires to be your friend?

You probably have an opinion about what the ideal friend looks like. You may want your friends to be loyal and supportive, to make time for you, and to listen to your problems. Make a list below of the qualities you want in a friend. Then consider how God fulfills your deepest need for friendship.

How can you be an ideal friend to God?

Pray the following:
God, thank You for the promise that You will always remain with me. I want to remain with You and enjoy real friendship with You. Help me to make the choice each day to be in Your presence and to stay close to You. Amen.

MAINTAIN YOUR DEPENDENCE

READ JOHN 15:5.

"I am the vine; you are the branches. The one who remains in me and I in him produces much fruit, because you can do nothing without me."
— John 15:5

DISCOVER

If you're like most people, it probably feels like you've worked your entire life to gain your independence. You've fought for it. At times, maybe you clashed with your parents to achieve it. You learned to do things on your own: walking, running, riding a bike, driving a car. Now, you're stepping into a whole new phase of independence. It's exciting to think about everything that lies ahead! Maybe you're moving into your own place, going to college, or starting a career. It probably feels like a final step toward your independence. But here's the truth: you'll never be fully independent. You aren't designed for it.

God created you to need Him. Jesus reminded the disciples of this truth in verse 5. There are a few things we can take from Jesus's words. First, Jesus wants us to remember our place. He is the vine, our source of life. He is our way to the Father, and we are completely dependent on Him for salvation because our own goodness will never be enough. Next, this verse reminds us that we can't grow without Him. The branch is completely dependent on the vine; it can't produce fruit if it's detached from the vine. It would dry up and whither. If we detach from Jesus, the same thing happens to us: when we wander from Him and try to live independently of Him, we fail to grow spiritually and produce fruit. We must remain attached to the Vine if we want to live abundant, full lives.

As you step toward more freedom, remember Jesus's words. We can't produce fruit on our own; we can't be "good enough" on our own. Christ is our vine, and we thrive when we stay connected to Him. As you walk in more independence, maintain your dependence on Jesus.

When have you tried to be "good enough" on your own? Why do our efforts to be "good enough" fail?

How does our culture push us to be independent from God? In what ways can you practice being completely dependent on Him?

Read Galatians 5:22-23. Which of these qualities of the fruit of the Spirit do you see growing in your own life? Which ones aren't? As believers, we are in the process of becoming more like Jesus. God doesn't expect us to instantly have all of these qualities, but He does empower us to develop them as we walk with Him. Intimacy with God will produce these qualities in us. In the chart below, note which qualities you are growing in and which you are not. Pray about why you're not growing in these areas and ask God to help you.

FRUIT	GROWING OR NOT GROWING?
Love	
Joy	
Peace	
Patience	
Kindness	
Goodness	
Faithfulness	
Gentleness	
Self Control	

Pray the following:
God, help me remember to depend on You. Help me to always know that true life comes from You. Any good fruit in my life is because I am connected to You, the true vine. When I am tempted to wander or to live independently of You, remind me of my great need for You. Thank You that I can do nothing on my own. Draw me closer to You. Amen.

A HEART LIKE HIS

READ JOHN 15:6-8.

*"If you remain in me and my words remain in you,
ask whatever you want and it will be done for you."*
— John 15:7

DISCOVER

Do you ever wish you had a magic lamp that would grant you three wishes—whatever you wanted? (Except for more wishes, of course!) Jesus says that those who remain in Him should "ask whatever you want, and it will be done for you" (John 15:7). Some might read this and start to tell God everything they ever wanted, thinking that He will give it to them immediately and in exactly they way they want, just like a magic genie. Others who read this may have given up on prayer, thinking, *I've already asked God for so many things and He never answered!* No matter your story or where you're coming from, know this: God deeply cares about you, your heart, and your desires.

But praying isn't the secret to getting whatever we want or an excuse to view God's role in our life as nothing more than a wish granter. What Jesus is saying here is that when you remain in Him and His Word remains in you, the things you ask for and the desires of your heart will begin to reflect His desires and His heart. That is what He wants: for your heart to look like His!

The more you grow in Jesus, the more you will want to be like Him and the more you will begin to trust Him. You will learn to trust God even when He says "no" or "wait." You will know that in His sovereignty, He does what He chooses for your good and His glory. This trust is so different from the way the world tends to act, it can be the very thing that allows others to see that you are a disciple of Jesus and see the fruit that comes from being in a relationship with Him!

What role does prayer play in your life? Why? How can you treat prayer less like a way to get God to give you what you want and more like a way for you to grow closer to Him?

According to verse 8, how can God be glorified in your life? How can you be diligent in glorifying God in this way as you enter a new phase of your life?

Make a list of all the things you have been praying for recently. Take some time to read over this list and think about how it reflects your heart and the way that you view God. Are your prayers honoring the Lord? Are you holding back because you might think God doesn't care about your heart's desires? Are you willing to surrender this list to the Lord and trust that He knows best?

Pray the following:
God, thank You for caring about me so deeply and caring about my heart. Help me to remember that You are my Father and to come to You with all things. Reveal to me the things that are not honoring to You. Make me more like You and align my heart with Yours. Amen.

MORE THAN JUST RULES

READ JOHN 15:9-10.

"If you keep my commands you will remain in my love, just as I have kept my Father's commands and remain in his love."
— John 15:10

DISCOVER

As kids, we often see rules and boundaries as restrictive and unfair. But as we grow up, we can see that what once looked cruel was put there for our protection by the people who love and care about us.

The same thing may be true about how we view the commandments given to us in Scripture. We might think that following Jesus is all about rules and that He doesn't want us to experience life to the fullest. In reality, when Jesus gave His followers commands, He did so because of His love for us and the love that the Father has for His creation. That is what it truly means to live life to the fullest: living a life connected to God.

Remember, Jesus called us to "remain" because God—our Creator—desires to have a deep and personal relationship with us. We don't keep His commandments to earn His love—we keep His commandments out of the love He has for us. In His love, we find joy, freedom, and purpose. Jesus paved the way and set the perfect example of keeping the Father's commandments. As humans, we will fail and make mistakes, but as disciples of Jesus, we are renewed daily and invited into the love that Christ so lavishly pours on us—the very same love that the Father pours out on the Son.

How does the Father love the Son? How do you know?

How have you seen the love of the Father in your own life?

Take time to write out how you have seen God's love and protection through being obedient to His commandments. How have you seen disobedience bring consequences to your life?

Pray the following:
God, remind me today of Your deep love for me. Remind me that You give Your commandments out of Your love for me. Remind me that You know what is best for me, and thank You for loving me in spite of my past failures. Amen.

JOY IN OBEDIENCE

READ JOHN 15:11.

*"I have told you these things so that my joy may be in you
and your joy may be complete."*
— John 15:11

DISCOVER

Everything Jesus had taught His disciples up to this verse was for the purpose of producing joy. And not just joy that appears out of nowhere— joy that comes from being obedient to everything we have talked about over the last few days. We are not called to reluctant rule-following but to joyful and faithful service. Choosing to joyfully follow Jesus is how we remain in Him, even though it means forsaking our own worldly wants and desires to pursue Him. The result of remaining in Christ and letting Him be the focus and priority of our lives will be having His joy.

We live in a world that encourages us to focus on ourselves and on doing what is in our best interest without considering others. But there is true joy found in following Jesus and serving others. Being obedient isn't always easy. In fact, it will often be difficult. Jesus Himself demonstrated this through obeying the Father to the point of giving His life for us on the cross! But through His obedience, Jesus found joy, and when we follow Him, we too will find a joy that can't be experienced outside of Him. It is through Christ alone that we can learn to lay down our own lives to be made complete in Him.

In this next season of life, you will be bombarded more than ever with many different views on what it means to have joy. Remember: there is no true joy apart from Jesus, no matter what the world says. Hold fast to the truths you have learned so far in John 15. All that Christ has done and instructed is for you to experience the fullness of life in Him and Him alone!

Why do you think joy is a result of being obedient to God's commandments? How have you experienced this joy?

Do you truly believe that Jesus could have joy even while facing death on the cross? Why or why not?

Write about a time when you joyfully sacrificed your wants or plans to genuinely serve someone else. Regardless of whether you have experienced something like this, think of one way you can give up your preferences or plans to serve someone else this week.

Pray the following:
Jesus, thank You for desiring to give me an unfailing joy. Thank You for setting the example for me to follow and for grace when I fail. Help me to find ways to serve and love others the way You have served and loved me. Allow the joy You give me to be a testimony to share about You and Your goodness. Amen.

JOHN 15:5

MEMORY VERSE

"I am the vine; you are the branches. The one who remains in me and I in him produces much fruit, because you can do nothing without me."
— John 15:5

LOVE IS A VERB

READ JOHN 15:12-13.

"This is my command: Love one another as I have loved you. No one has greater love than this: to lay down his life for his friends."
— John 15:12-13

DISCOVER

As I sit down to write today, Chopin's Piano Concerto No. 1 is playing in the background. It's one of my favorite pieces both to listen to and to play. The second movement particularly reminds me of love and romance and all the beautiful things associated with them.

In our key verses today, Jesus talks about love, but perhaps not in the way depicted in any of our favorite romantic songs: He *commands* us to love. Throughout the Bible, we learn that God is love. So, commanding us to love may sound strange or even harsh. After all, how do we command our emotions to love someone?

Jesus is reminding us that love is not just about emotions—it's about action. Two chapters prior, in John 13, Jesus showed love by washing His disciples' feet, even though He knew that the very next day, He would be betrayed by one of them, denied by another, abandoned by the rest (except for John), and be killed. Yet, what was on His mind was love.

Love was also on His mind as He willingly went to the cross to die for us so that we could be reconciled to Him. Jesus laid down His own life for those who followed Him and loved Him, as well as for those who rejected and despised Him. As He loved, He calls us to love by serving one another and putting love into action.

In Scripture, how do we see Jesus show that love is more than an emotion?

What is difficult about Jesus's commandment for us to love one another?

What are some ways God has shown you that He loves you? What are some ways you can show love through action? Ask God to show you who needs to be shown His love today, and ask Him how to show it. This could be as simple as sending a text or lending a listening ear. As Jesus loved us, so we are called to show His love to others.

As you pray today, thank God that He is love and He loves us unconditionally. Thank Him for all the ways He shows us His love, including sending His Son, Jesus, to die on the cross for us. Ask Him to open your eyes to see who needs to be shown His love.

FRIEND OF GOD

READ JOHN 15:14-15.

"You are my friends if you do what I command you. I do not call you servants anymore, because a servant doesn't know what his master is doing. I have called you friends, because I have made known to you everything I have heard from my Father."
— John 15:14-15

DISCOVER

"Because I said so!" When you were younger, did your parents ever respond with this statement after you questioned one of their rules or instructions? Mine sure did. Such a statement reveals a clear parent-child relationship. Parents don't owe their kids an explanation for all of their instructions.

Friends, however, do share their intentions and thoughts. In these verses, Jesus is shifting from master-servant language to the language of friendship. As His death approached, Jesus drew the disciples closer to Himself. He took them behind the curtain, so to speak, offering insight into His relationship with God (see John 15:9) and what God desired for them. He gave them all the remaining information they needed to follow Him, and He told them to "remain in [His] love" and to "love one another as [He] loved [them]" (John 15:9-12). They could no longer claim ignorance as an excuse for not following His teachings.

To be considered a friend of Jesus, one must follow His commands—and obedience is a result of one's faith in Jesus. Rather than blindly obeying Him, a believer follows Jesus because they love Him. Jesus offers this friendship to all believers, not just His original disciples. This means Jesus, the One who laid down His life for His friends, is asking you to be His friend, too.

Would you consider yourself a friend of Jesus? Why or why not?

What are some ways you can be a better friend to Jesus?

What are some ways you can continue to cultivate friendship with Jesus in the next part of your life?

Think of some of your friends. What makes them good friends? Are they trustworthy, loyal, caring, and supportive? It's always nice to have good friends we can count on. When we use the language of friendship to describe our relationship with Jesus, it is also describing our relationship with God, the ultimate supporter and provider. Think about how you would describe Jesus, your friend. Below write attributes that describe who Jesus is.

Thank God for His friendship with you. Ask Him to forgive you for where you have fallen short. Pray that you would remain close to Him and that you would be given the opportunity to share Jesus with friends of yours who do not know Him.

LASTING FRUIT

READ JOHN 15:16-17.

*"You did not choose me, but I chose you. I appointed you to go
and produce fruit and that your fruit should remain, so that
whatever you ask the Father in my name, he will give you.
This is what I command you: Love one another."*
— John 15:16-17

DISCOVER

Think of your favorite fruit. Perhaps it's a sweet strawberry or a peach.
Now think of a spoiled fruit you can no longer enjoy. No one likes spoiled
fruit, right? It smells, it's covered in mold, and it's no longer good to eat.
In these verses, Jesus is focused on fruit that lasts and never spoils. He
wants His followers to remain in Him and produce good fruit.

In verse 16, Jesus reminds His disciples they are in relationship with
Him because He appointed them and set them apart. This relationship
wasn't because of any achievement of their own—the disciples were
simply recipients of God's grace. While Jesus may have also told them
this to keep their egos in check, He ultimately told them His reason for
appointing them: to bear fruit that lasts.

Jesus has chosen you and is calling you to bear lasting fruit as well. He
wants you to continue to place your faith in Him and obey His commands.
Wherever you go, seek to be set apart from the world. Rather than being
solely focused on yourself as the world demands, seek opportunities to
love others and share the gospel. Be confident in Christ's love for you
and allow His love to pour out to others. Through your acts of love, you
will be a witness for Jesus. And remember, Jesus hasn't given you this
mission and just left you on your own: He remains with you. Through it all,
you can turn to God in prayer.

How does it feel to know Jesus has chosen you? How does it give you confidence to live out your faith?

What are some ways you can tell that someone is bearing good fruit? How do they act and treat others?

Bear fruit that remains—that lasts. God is not interested in a temporary fix. He sent Jesus to die so that we may be reconciled to Him for eternity. Similarly, Jesus wants us to remain in Him and make a lasting impact on others through the way we love. How can we do this? We do this by continuously demonstrating love for others. Is there someone who has consistently loved you? Think of how you can share the love of Jesus with this person. And if there is someone with whom you have shared the gospel, follow up with her or him. Walk beside this person, answer questions, and pray together as she or he learns who Jesus is.

Pray the following:
God, thank You for choosing me and sending Your Son, Jesus, to die for my sins. Help me to be the person You designed me to be, one who remains in You and shares Your love with those around me. Amen.

NOT OF THIS WORLD

READ JOHN 15:18-19

*"If the world hates you, understand that it hated me before it
hated you. If you were of the world, the world would love you
as its own. However, because you are not of the world,
but I have chosen you out of it, the world hates you."*
— John 15:18-19

DISCOVER

In these verses, Jesus is speaking with His disciples about what their lives
would be like after He was gone. Specifically, He's telling them what it
would look like if the disciples used their lives to share the gospel with
the lost of the world. Jesus wanted His disciples to know that being a
Christian means living life differently than the world, which might result
in the world "hating" them. But there would comfort for the disciples in
knowing that Jesus had walked this path before they did. They would not
be alone.

In verse 19, Jesus reminds the disciples that they should be different
in the way they speak and act. This might draw attention to them—the
world does not always respond kindly to those who speak and act on
Jesus's behalf. So they shouldn't be surprised; this is just how the world
often responds to the upside-down message of the gospel.

As Christians today, our lives should also look different, even if this results
in the world "hating" us. One of the most apparent examples of this is
the way believers are treated in countries where Christianity is banned.
Believers are hated by the governments of those countries and are often
prosecuted for their faith. For others of us, this could look like losing
relationships with friends or family members as a result of sharing the
gospel or living and believing according to the Bible. There's good news,
though: when we share about Jesus and His teachings, some of the lost
will come to know Him as their Lord and Savior! This is why we share
about Jesus and His gospel.

Do you see yourself as loved or hated by the world? How so?

If you were to speak and act according to Jesus's teachings, how could the world respond to you?

As you enter a new stage of life, how can you continue to live for Jesus, even if it means hatred from the world?

This Scripture can be intimidating to read and think about how it applies to life. Who enjoys being hated by anyone? But if Jesus gave us this teaching, then there must be good that comes from following Him and sharing His teachings with the world. Take a moment and list some ways you can share about Jesus and His teachings with the people in your life who don't know Him. Take a moment and list some ways the world may respond when you do this.

Ways I Can Share About Jesus and His Teachings	Ways the World May Respond

Instead of praying that God will spare you from the world's hatred, pray that God would be with you as you speak and follow Christ's example in the world. Pray that the Lord would go before you and prepare people's hearts to respond to Jesus's teachings with acceptance of the gospel and life change. Pray the Lord will give you strength when some do not accept these things and instead respond with hate.

PERSECUTED LIKE CHRIST

READ JOHN 15:20-21

"Remember the word I spoke to you: 'A servant is not greater than his master.' If they persecuted me, they will also persecute you. If they kept my word, they will also keep yours. But they will do all these things to you on account of my name, because they don't know the one who sent me."
— John 15:20-21

DISCOVER

In verse 20, Jesus points His disciples back to one of His previous teachings, when He said, "A servant is not greater than his master, and a messenger is not greater than the one who sent him" (John 13:16-18). The job of a servant and a messenger is to complete the mission of the master or sender. Therefore, if the master or sender is persecuted, his servants or messengers will most likely be as well. This is applicable to Jesus's disciples and followers both in ancient times and today.

Jesus continues by giving encouragement to the disciples, explaining to them that those who also believe in Him and follow Him after hearing His message through the disciples will keep His teachings as well.

Then Jesus points back to what He said about persecution: the lost respond the way they do because they do not know Jesus as their Lord and Savior. A saying I have heard before is that we shouldn't expect lost people to act saved. Why? Because they haven't come to know Jesus as their Lord and Savior yet. This seems simple enough when you think about it, but as Christians, we continue to be surprised when the lost of the world act like the world in their response to Christians and the news of the gospel. Jesus explains that this is to be expected. Instead of being surprised by the actions and attitudes of the lost, let's see them the way Jesus does and love these people like He does.

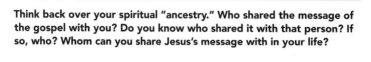

Think back over your spiritual "ancestry." Who shared the message of the gospel with you? Do you know who shared it with that person? If so, who? Whom can you share Jesus's message with in your life?

Jesus told the disciples that people would persecute them "because they don't know the one who sent [Him]" (v. 21). How could this change the way you approach unbelievers?

When people who don't know Jesus yet respond poorly to you, does it give you empathy for them when you remember that they don't yet have the hope of salvation that you have? Why or why not?

Jesus didn't explain that His disciples would be persecuted to cause us to fear sharing about Him and the gospel. Can you identify two or three things that God is calling you to share about or do that may cause persecution or discomfort in your life?

Let's create a plan of accountability. Whom in your life can you talk to about these things to find encouragement and support in the face of persecution, frustration, or discomfort?

Pray that God would give you a spirit of boldness as you follow through on the action steps you listed above. Pray that the Lord will give you a community of believers who will support and encourage you. Pray that the Lord will open your eyes to new ways to share the gospel with the world.

NO EXCUSE

READ JOHN 15:22-25

*"If I had not come and spoken to them, they would not be guilty of sin.
Now they have no excuse for their sin."*
— John 15:22

DISCOVER

Chances are, you've already encountered people who oppose the truth of Jesus. If you haven't, I'm certain that soon you will meet people who are apathetic to their need for Christ and others who stand in direct opposition to Him.

Because Jesus was sinless, His life revealed the sin in the lives of those He encountered. People who didn't know Jesus also didn't know God the Father. The same is true today: looking at our lives compared to sinless Jesus reveals our sinful state.

When your life reflects Jesus, you can expect that some people who see the truth of Christ lived out will experience the guilt of their sin. Hopefully, some will be convicted and come to faith Jesus.

As you move into the next season of life, you will experience many transitions, possibly including a new school, a new job, a new home, new friends, a new church, and a new community. As you begin this new journey, I would like to encourage you to:

- Be bold.
- Stand for truth in all aspects of your life.
- Speak the gospel clearly but gracefully.
- Be expectant for God to move in your life.
- Know that persecution will come as a response to truth.
- Pray for chances to share the gospel with those who oppose Jesus.

How does looking at Jesus reveal your own sinful nature?

Have you ever experienced persecution, difficulty, or discomfort for sharing your faith in Christ? What happened?

How can you continue to share the gospel with others even when there is opposition?

You have many upcoming transitions. Circle the transitions below that you anticipate. Feel free to add to the list if needed.

NEW JOB

NEW SCHOOL (SUCH
AS COLLEGE OR
TECHNICAL SCHOOL)

MOVING AWAY
FROM HOME

MAKING NEW
FRIENDS

FINDING A NEW
CHURCH

NEW RESPONSIBILITIES

List two to three ways you can prepare now to boldly proclaim the truth as you enter this new season and face these life transitions.

Spend time in prayer asking God to prepare you for the upcoming transitions that you identified above. Ask Him for boldness as you seek to live your life to honor Him. May you be expectant for how He will continue to shape your heart and the hearts of those with whom you have the opportunity to share the truth.

TESTIFY

READ JOHN 15:26-27.

"You also will testify, because you have been with me from the beginning."
— John 15:27

DISCOVER

As you graduate and take your next steps, many things may change for you. You may find that you have to rely more on yourself than you did in high school because you're taking on new responsibilities and becoming more independent. So in your spiritual walk, as you find opportunities to share Jesus with others, you may be tempted to do so from your own strength.

The Holy Spirit is a gift from God, the third Person of the Trinity. Through Him, God dwells with us after Jesus returned to the right-hand side of the Father. He is the "Spirit of truth" (v. 26) and He testifies about Jesus just as today's verses describe. To "testify" means to give evidence of something. When you give your life to Christ in faith, you are given the gift of the Holy Spirit to live inside of you, guiding you into all truth (see John 16:13) and helping you testify to what God has done in your life.

As you were challenged yesterday to expectantly look for opportunities to share the truth of the gospel, you can confidently trust that the Holy Spirit will be the One to speak through you. It is only by His power that others will come to know Him—this is not a task that you can take on successfully alone. So humbly accept the gift of the Holy Spirit in your life and rely on Him to guide you. As you share about Jesus and boldly live a life that is honoring to Him, the Holy Spirit will be at work speaking truth into the lives of the people with whom you share.

Have you seen the work of the Holy Spirit in your life? If so, how? If not, what are some ways that He might be working?

What is something that could be keeping you from listening to the Holy Spirit or obeying Him?

As you go throughout your day, trust the Holy Spirit to work through you as you interact with others. Ask the Lord to place people before you with whom you can share your life and the gospel. Remember, your life reflects the work of Jesus within you. May it be honorable and bring glory to Him.

Pray the following:
Dear God, I thank You for the gift of the Holy Spirit in my life. What an encouragement it is to know that You are with me as I go! Help me to trust the power of the Holy Spirit speaking truth through me. Open my eyes to see those You place before me who need to hear the life-changing truth of the gospel and give me the boldness to speak. Amen.

"God delights to share his power with those who are bold enough to bother him." — J. D. Greear[4]

"Whatever else you do, do the only thing that can make you feel truly alive—do life with Christ." — Rachel Jones[5]

"Stand your ground. And always do so with kindness. It's the combination of these two things that is so powerful." — Michael J. Kruger[6]

"Discerning God's calling is more a relationship than a route, more journey than destination. It's about who you are becoming more than where you are going. Perhaps it's less about what you do and more about how well you do whatever you do." — Levi Lusko[7]

"Faith does not eliminate questions. But faith knows where to take them." — Elisabeth Elliot[8]

"For the LORD gives wisdom; from his mouth come knowledge and understanding." — Proverbs 2:6

"For as heaven is higher than earth, so my ways are higher than your ways, and my thoughts than your thoughts." — Isaiah 55:9

"'Peace I leave with you. My peace I give to you. I do not give to you as the world gives. Don't let your heart be troubled or fearful.'" — John 14:27

"Who among you is wise and understanding? By his good conduct he should show that his works are done in the gentleness that comes from wisdom." — James 3:13

"Wisdom from above is first pure, then peace-loving, gentle, compliant, full of mercy and good fruits, unwavering, without pretense." — James 3:17

EPHESIANS 3:14-21

Can you imagine what it would have felt like to be prayed for by the apostle Paul? In Ephesians 3:14-21, Paul offers a prayer for the church in Ephesus that echoes all the way to today. What he prays for is exactly what you need as you move to a new phase in life. It's as if two thousand years ago, Paul was praying for you!

WRITERS:

Taylor Heatherly (Days 23–25)
Event Coordinator, FUGE Camps

Tega Faafa Taylor (Days 26–28)
Brand Owner/Content Editor, Hyfi Students

Kyle Cravens (Days 29–30)
Team Leader, FUGE Camps

THE POSTURE OF MY LIFE

READ EPHESIANS 3:14-15.

*For this reason I kneel before the Father from whom
every family in heaven and on earth is named.*
— Ephesians 3:14-15

DISCOVER

Have you ever wondered why people sometimes kneel during prayer? The significance of kneeling during prayer is as simple as this—it is a posture of humility and complete surrender towards God. We see this in verse 14 as Paul, a humble servant, prays for God to give strength that only He can provide. Paul was demonstrating what it means to be completely surrendered to God. The glory of God brought him quite literally to his knees.

Verse 15 shows us the magnitude of who God really is—He is Father over all. It says that He is the One "from whom every family in heaven and on earth is named." Have you ever thought about the fact that this includes you? The Creator of the universe created you and invites you to call Him Father. There is no greater honor in this life than getting to kneel before the Father, knowing that Jesus sacrificed it all to bring us this opportunity.

By treating God like the magnificent Father He is, we experience the magnitude of what God has done for us. Kneeling before the Father is a symbol of our obedience, an acknowledgment that He is King, and a way of expressing our desire for Him to continue to have His way in our life. In kneeling before the Father, we submit our will to His.

Reflect on your personal journey. When was a time you experienced God so powerfully that it physically brought you to your knees?

How were you changed after experiencing God in this way?

How does the posture of your life reflect a life surrendered to following Jesus, wherever He leads?

When you read these verses, they can come across as subtle. However, I think there is much power in submitting to the words of these verses. God is the only One who deserves our praise. He is the only One we should be bowing before. He should be the greatest object of affection in our lives. But there are many different ways that we can display our love for and surrender to Jesus. In the space below, write down some other ways that you can show your complete surrender to the Lord.

Your surrender and obedience could be just what someone in your class, your dorm, or your intramural sport needs to take the next step in his or her journey. Pray that God would reveal Himself to you in brand new ways and that you would be obedient to the Holy Spirit in those moments. Ask God to remind you of the surrender and sacrifice of Jesus and pray that He would use you to reach the next person He is calling into His family.

SPIRITUAL STRENGTH AND POWER

READ EPHESIANS 3:14-16.

I pray that he may grant you, according to the riches of his glory, to be strengthened with power in your inner being through his Spirit . . .
— Ephesians 3:16

DISCOVER

Raise your hand if anyone has ever told you that life post-graduation would be easy and that you would never have any hardships or troubles as you step into adulthood. Hopefully your hand isn't in the air! I think we can all agree that this isn't true. You're entering a transitional season of your life, and often that will bring tough decisions and new struggles. We cannot rely on our own strength to carry us through to the end at these kinds of times.

In verse 16, Paul is calling on the unlimited and never-ending riches of the Lord to strengthen and equip us. One thing I think is significant to acknowledge is that Paul asks for strength from God through the Holy Spirit. God gave us the Holy Spirit as an immediate resource and Advocate who provides closeness in our times of need. Through the Holy Spirit, we have God's power within us.

There is no strength and no power like the Lord's. So, when the "adulting" starts to pick up and you feel overwhelmed and unequipped, let this be a reminder to you that you have access to a spiritual power within you. The way you battle trials in the spiritual world directly affects how you overcome them in the natural world. This is why we must humbly posture ourselves towards God, knowing that His way for us is the way to joy. And following this way requires devotion and complete trust in the One who is strong enough to hold it all.

Do you typically find yourself relying on your own strength or on strength from God when it comes to trials and tribulations? Why?

What is an area of your life that you want God to help strengthen you through?

Paul's ministry is a great example of how to humbly and confidently walk through life while relying on the empowerment of the Spirit. As you go through the rest of your day, take a moment to ask God to fuel you, and make it a point to acknowledge the work of the Holy Spirit in your life.

Pray the following:

Father, thank You for Your closeness each and every day. In the times when I am scared, worried, stressed, confused, or overwhelmed, You never fail to be in complete control. You are the ultimate Source of strength I need as I face each day. Lord, teach me how to be more sensitive to the Spirit and how You are moving within my heart. I want to trust Your power, Your presence, and Your strength more today than I did yesterday, and more tomorrow than I do today. I trust You, Lord. Amen.

NEW HOME

READ EPHESIANS 3:14-17a.

. . .and that Christ may dwell in your hearts through faith.
— Ephesians 3:17a

DISCOVER

Have you ever thought about the saying "home is where the heart is"? The place you call home most likely is the place where your fondest memories were made, where your love for your friends and family developed, and where you feel the safest. We all like to feel safe. We all like to feel seen, known, and loved—and "home" typically is where we feel that the most.

As you take this next step in your journey, there is a chance you may be leaving the place that you've called "home" for a very long time. Some of you may be packing your things to move to a completely new city. Some of you may be planning to just go a few minutes down the road, surrounding yourself with new community that you've never experienced before. Home might be starting to look different for you.

Although you may be up and moving to a new city, a new space, a new school, a new normal—in short, a new home—you have full access to the Father through your faith in Jesus. As believers, He has made His "home" within your heart. How grateful are you to know that God has made your heart a home for Himself?

As you invite Jesus into your next season, would you trust Him with your all? Just as home is the place where you feel the most seen, known, and loved, the Lord is on this journey with you. He is already working to make this new place home for you. And in this new place, He wants you to dwell in Him, just as He dwells within you.

When you think about stepping into your new "home" as you move into the next season of your life, what are some things you are nervous about?

How can you invite Christ into those new spaces with you?

Who are some people who can keep you accountable and remind you to trust Jesus with some of these areas you're nervous about?

In order for a home to stay standing, it needs to have a firm foundation. In order for a home to feel safe, the walls and roof need to be intact. Use the space below draw a house and write "Jesus" at the bottom. Use this as a reminder that Christ is the strongest foundation for you to build your life on. When you get the foundation right, the walls and roof are sure to stand—even in new and unfamiliar places.

Take a moment to pray that God would bring you exactly the peace and comfort you need as you prepare to make this new season of life "home." Ask Him to multiply your faith today as you trust in Him for a God-honoring community, friendships, church, and outreach opportunities. Thank Him for dwelling within your heart and making it a home within you. Pray that you may experience the fullness of who He is through each and every encounter with His Spirit.

ROOTS OF LOVE

READ EPHESIANS 3:14-17.

I pray that you, being rooted and firmly established in love . . .
— Ephesians 3:17b

DISCOVER

Have you ever looked out in nature and been amazed by the size of the trees around you? If you've ever witnessed a beautiful grove of towering trees, you know that the strongest trees require the strongest roots. Roots are important for the tree to gain nutrients, water, and most importantly, to anchor the tree to the ground. Without strong roots, a tree will topple in the midst of stress, storms, and waterless seasons.

In his letter to the Ephesian church, Paul compares us to a tree, reminding us of the importance of being rooted and firmly established. Like a tree, it's pivotal that we have a strong foundation—but not just any foundation. Paul clarifies that this foundation must be in love. Not only does this foundation sustain us, but it keeps us grounded in the midst of the storms of life. Whether you face friendships changing, are grieving the loss of the comfort of high school, are confused about your next step, or are even insecure because you're not where someone else is, love will keep you going.

Having roots that are based in love isn't an automatic thing. Desiring a strong relationship with Jesus as the foundation for all things isn't our natural inclination—it's a relationship we must nurture and continually mature into. Paul prayed this for the Ephesian church. The question is, who is praying this for you? The people who have loved and mentored you to this point are continuing to pray for you as you move into this new stage in life. Who will be the ones to help you be rooted in love in the next?

How do you feel about unexpected change? Why?

What's a storm—a challenging experience—that you've walked through recently? How did this storm affect you?

What steps can you take to begin to develop roots of love for the next season of your life?

For a tree to grow strong roots, three things are required: water, oxygen, and space. In order for us to weather the storms of life, we must also create systems to grow. Fill out the following chart to create a spiritual root growth plan. Use the italicized questions to prompt thinking.

What I Need:	My Spiritual Growth Plan
WATER Are there areas of your faith that have been in a drought season? What are attributes of God that you can be reminded of in times of drought?	
OXYGEN *Exhale* — What are things that you may need to confess to God and/or your community? *Inhale* — What are areas of your life where you can trust that the Holy Spirit is in control?	
SPACE How often do you create space for Jesus in your day? Where are places you need to look in your new phase in life for faith community that will nurture you in love? What are intentional environments you can be in that can help you grow?	

If you can, go outside to an area with trees, such as a local park, a botanical garden, or even your backyard. Take time to sit and marvel. Thank God for the strength and steadiness of trees. Pray that He grows your roots to be strong in love for Him and others due to an overflowing love from Jesus.

MEMORY VERSES

I pray that you, being **rooted and firmly established in love,** may be able to comprehend with all the saints what **is the length and width, height and depth of God's love,** and to know Christ's love that surpasses knowledge, **so that you may be filled with all the fullness of God.**

Ephesians 3:17b-19

IMMEASURABLY MORE

READ EPHESIANS 3:14-18.

. . . may be able to comprehend with all the saints what is the length and width, height and depth of God's love . . .
— Ephesians 3:18

DISCOVER

When you hear the word "expectations," what's the first thing you think of? Expectations are the strong belief that something will (or should) go one way or another, and they're normally based on what we've experienced in our lives. For many of us, when it comes to life after high school, the expectation is that all the pieces will be in place and the entire story that God is unfolding will be clear.

Unfortunately, that isn't often our reality. There are usually many missing pieces and unanswered questions. *What will next few years hold? Who will I meet? Will life go according to my plan? What if things don't work out? Will I still be dating the same person? Will friendships last?*

With all these questions, it can be difficult to see the masterpiece God is unfolding or even who He is in the midst of the mystery—and Paul knew this would happen. In Ephesians 3:18, he prays that we "may be able to comprehend" the magnitude of God's love—that we may be able to understand God in full, even when we don't understand the full picture.

Read the verse closely—this understanding of God isn't done alone. Paul urges that we may be able to understand the greatness of God's love "with all the saints." The key word here is "all." This includes the old and the young, the rich and the poor, and people of all different races, ethnicities, and backgrounds pointing toward the same person: Jesus. As an individual, we may not always be able to see the full picture, but together, our experiences reveal that our God is so much bigger, so much deeper, and so much more than we know.

Reflect on a time when you struggled to see the fullness of God's love. What happened?

Why are multiple perspectives of God's love important for understanding God?

The love of God is immeasurable, yet Paul uses words that we use for making measurements. Why do you think he does this?

Consider the "immeasurably more" aspect of the length, width, height, and depth of God's love. Answer the questions in the space provided below or in a journal, using stories and experiences from your own life and people you may know.

When was a time you realized that God's love is limitless?

When was a time you realized that God's love includes all people?

When was a time you realized that God's love is higher than the love of anyone else?

When was a time in which you realized the strength and richness of God's love?

Take time to reflect on the boxes you may put God in.
Acknowledge the pieces of your life that may be limiting you from seeing and experiencing the fullness of God. Ask Him to show you the "immeasurably more" love He has for you.

EMBRACING THE UNKNOWN

READ EPHESIANS 3:14-19.

*. . . and to know Christ's love that surpasses knowledge, so that you may
be filled with all the fullness of God.*
— Ephesians 3:19

DISCOVER

"I don't know."

Just reading that probably made you feel certain thoughts and emotions.
Answering a question "I don't know" is often frowned upon and viewed
as a lack of intelligence or lack of insight. In the age of social media,
search engines, and a plethora of knowledge at our fingertips, it's difficult
to admit that there's an unknown. In your life right now, stepping into
what's next probably feels as though there's so much unknown.

In Ephesians 3:19, Paul reminds us that in the midst of what is unknown,
there's one thing we can be confidently sure of—Christ's love. In fact, this
love is so grand that it surpasses all knowledge. It surpasses the plans
we may have for what's ahead. It surpasses the fears and doubts we may
have about our futures. This love even surpasses the very things we don't
know! In turn, this love that surpasses what we both know and don't know
isn't just something that keeps us comfortable. Truly, this love changes
us. It changes us so much that we walk differently, talk differently, and
live differently.

Whether you need to be filled with peace, security, confidence, joy,
assurance, healing, or all of the above—and regardless of what may be
ahead of you—God is right beside you. His love expands and extends
beyond this very moment, reminding you that in the midst of what's next
and what's passed, He is with you. Always.

Fill out the following chart for what you do and don't know about the coming year.

What I Know:	What's Unknown:	What I Know About God:

How can God's love shift your perspective on the unknown areas of your life?

Write a letter to the future you. In the letter, specifically talk through the anticipation, excitement, fears, and unknowns you may have at this point in your life. Put the letter in an envelope and date it to be opened nine months from when you wrote it. You'll be amazed at what God does between now and then!

Take time to pray over your letter and speak with God honestly. Thank Him for the fact that His love surpasses all that is known and unknown. As you pray, take time to breathe and be reminded of the One who is faithful, sovereign, and able.

ABOVE AND BEYOND

READ EPHESIANS 3:14-20.

Now to him who is able to do above and beyond all that we ask or think according to the power that works in us . . .
— Ephesians 3:20

DISCOVER

The past couple of years have held some major decisions and milestones for you. You have doubtless spent much time looking to the future and what it holds for you. Where has God been in your decision making and in your future? How much time have you spent in prayer about this year and the upcoming transition?

Paul tells us that God is "able to do above and beyond all that we ask or think" (v. 20). God loves us and has a purpose and plan for each of our lives. But we have to tap into Him in order to know His will, which means we have to ask. When we do, He will open doors and give us the ability to do whatever He wants us to do.

Often, the opportunities God gives us require courage, boldness, and trust. Sometimes, we're guilty of putting limits on God. Maybe we feel that we aren't good enough or qualified. Maybe we're scared of the unknown. Maybe we don't want to leave our comfort zones. When we put limits on God, we are essentially saying that we don't believe He can work in and through us.

At this crossroads in your life, the time is now to go all in! Try the impossible. Take risks. Allow your faith to take over. Realize that you have a whole world in front of you. Don't limit what God wants to do in your life. He is able. And He is available—always has been and always will be.

How would you describe your current feelings when it comes to graduating and looking to your future? Circle all that apply.

NERVOUS   ANXIOUS   EXCITED   WORRIED

CONFIDENT   COURAGEOUS   BRAVE

HOPEFUL   SAD

TRUSTING   AFRAID   UNCERTAIN

Write about these feelings below.

Do you honestly believe that God can do things in your life which are above and beyond what you ask or even think? Circle the answer below that fits best.

YES   No   UNCERTAIN

Why do you feel this way?

What could you possibly be hindering God from doing in your life? Why do you think you are limiting God in this way?

Change is inevitable. Some people do well with change while others struggle with it. Make a list of the changes that will be coming your way after graduation. Mark the ones that you feel good about with a check mark. Mark the ones you are anxious or concerned about with an X (you could also use a color code if you like).

Prepare a list of realistic next steps you can take this summer to tap into God, step out in faith and courage, and trust Him during this time of transition.

Spend some time praying over all of the changes on the list you made earlier, thanking God for all of them. For those with an X, ask the Lord to help you trust Him and give you courage and boldness as you face these changes. Share this list with a trusted friend or adult and ask this person to pray for you during your exciting time of change and new experiences.

ALL THE GLORY

READ EPHESIANS 3:14-21.

. . . to him be glory in the church and in Christ Jesus to all generations,
forever and ever. Amen.
— Ephesians 3:21

DISCOVER

When Paul wrote today's verse, he was on house arrest. But he wasn't spending his time complaining or blaming others. Instead, he chose a spontaneous outburst of worship and praise. Paul's whole life and ministry was to give God glory and to make Him known among all nations.

God is worthy of all glory and honor for so many reasons: who He is, His nature and characteristics, and what He has done in the lives of those who love Him. Take a minute to reflect on who God is to you. How has He shown up in your life?

You have worked hard over the past four years, but you didn't get to this point in your journey alone. Consider those who helped you get to this point. Parents. Family. Teachers. Small group leaders. Youth pastors. Friends. Ultimately, you are here because God planned this for your life and helped you get to this exciting milestone.

Often, we think of worshiping and praising God as something that only happens when we're gathered with other believers at a church building. Have you ever stopped to realize that worship can take place on a personal level? In fact, we should live our lives with an attitude of worship. In Colossians 3:17, Paul urges us to "do everything in the name of the Lord Jesus, giving thanks to God the Father through him." As you look to the future, may you do everything in a way that gives God the glory!

Below is just a short list of the many characteristics of God. Which of these have you experienced firsthand or mean the most to you? Circle a couple. Which of these characteristics do you need help adopting in your own life? Underline those.

WISE   GOOD   JUST   MERCIFUL   GRACIOUS   LOVING

HOLY   GLORIOUS   ETERNAL   RIGHTEOUS   TRUTH

COMFORTER   FATHER   SOVEREIGN   COUNSELOR

PEACE   HEALER   STRENGTH   ALL-KNOWING

ALL-POWERFUL   COMPASSIONATE   FORGIVING

PROVIDER   PROTECTOR

How do you rate your personal worship of God? Mark your answer on the scale below.

1
NON-EXISTENT

3
WHEN THINGS ARE GREAT

5
LIVING A LIFESTYLE OF WORSHIP

Why did you rate yourself this way? How can you grow in your personal worship of God in the next phase of your life?

Take some time to think back over the past twelve to thirteen years of your life and list major milestones and spiritual markers—times where you have seen God work in your life.

Think about the next few years of your life. What type of relationship with God do you want to have when this phase of life comes to a close? What steps can you take now to get there?

Read back through your list of milestones and spiritual markers. Take a few minutes to realize God's part in all of those things, and thank Him for providing in so many awesome ways. Ask God to help you surrender to His will so that you will have many more of these in the future.

Turning Points

If you were writing a story, you'd want to build up to something amazing that would change the trajectory of your character's life forever. This is called a *turning point*. Through this event or series of events, you present that character with a choice, and that choice changes the direction of his or her life.

We all make countless decisions throughout our lives, but only a few could probably be called turning points—the moments when we feel the weight of a decision that just might change everything. These moments might change who our friends are, the way we interact with our families, what school we attend, or the way we live our lives.

When we choose to follow Jesus, that is the most important turning point of our lives. We go from lives lived for ourselves, focused only on our own dreams and desires, to lives lived for Him, focused on His will and plan for our lives. Our words change, our thoughts change, our actions change. And our definition of wisdom takes a new spin.

You have probably heard a thousand voices telling you different ways you could or should live at each turning point in your life, and graduating from high school is likely no different. But here's the thing: your purpose isn't only about what you do right now, or even later. Your purpose is to live for Jesus wherever you are throughout your life.

His wisdom will carry you through whatever you might face today, tomorrow, or years into the future. When you don't understand exactly what His wisdom is telling you, lean in and ask the Holy Spirit to help you. The Holy Spirit Himself is God's promise that He will.

Carry God's wisdom with you, whether you're graduating or stepping into a job or still searching for what's next. Congratulations! We're proud of you and excited for what God will do in you next!

— Your friends at
    Lifeway Students

End Notes

Introduction

1. Ben Trueblood, *Within Reach: The Power of Small Changes in Keeping Students Connected* (Nashville, TN: Lifeway Press, 2018), 11.

Section 1

2. Jay Van Bavel and Dominic Packer, "Sick of Failing at Your New Year's Resolutions? There Is a Better Way," *TIME*, December 29, 2022, https://time.com/6243642/how-to-keep-new-years-resolutions-2/.

3. Richard R. Melick, *Philippians, Colossians, Philemon*, vol. 32, The New American Commentary (Nashville: Broadman & Holman Publishers, 1991), Logos Bible Software version, 66.

Section 2

4. J. D. Greear, *Just Ask: The Joy of Confident, Bold, Patient, Relentless, Shameless, Dependent, Grateful, Powerful, Expectant Prayer* (Charlotte, NC: Good Book Company, 2021), 27.

5. Rachel Jones, *Is This It?* (Charlotte, NC: Good Book Company, 2019), 39–40.

6. Michael J. Kruger, *Surviving Religion 101: Letters to a Christian Student on Keeping the Faith* (Wheaton, IL: Crossway, 2021), 63.

7. Levi Lusko, *Through the Eyes of a Lion: Facing Impossible Pain, Finding Incredible Power* (Nashville, TN: Thomas Nelson, 2015), 29.

8. Elisabeth Elliot, *A Chance to Die: The Life and Legacy of Amy Carmichael* (Old Tappan, NJ: Fleming H. Revell Company, 1987), 55.

Engage with God's Word.

lifeway.com/teendevotionals

☐ **WORDS OF WISDOM**

☐ **PIONEER & PERFECTOR**

☐ **WITH YOU**

☐ **ROMANS**

☐ **LOVE AND JUSTICE**

☐ **CALLED TO THIS**

☐ **GROWING IN GRATITUDE**

☐ **GOD WITH US**

☐ **MADE NEW**

☐ **LOVE WITH ALL YOUR HEART**

☐ **RISEN**

☐ **WISDOM, STATURE, AND FAVOR**